AF481234

GROWING MINDS
BOOKS

REFRAME

Dr. Isaiah Varisano

I fell down
and scraped
my knee

but it will feel
better in a few
minutes.

I can't read yet

but I can start to
learn about letters
and sounds.

I didn't win the
game

but I had fun
and learned
how to play.

It is time to wash
my hair

but if I close my
eyes it won't be
so bad.

I got water in
my eyes

but I can wipe
them with a
towel.

I don't know
how to catch a
ball yet

but I can ask
someone to
teach me.

I lost my toy

but I can look
for it.

My friends can't come over to play

but I can play
by myself.

I spilled on my
shirt

but I can
change into a
clean one.

It is time for
bed

but tomorrow
will be another
great day.

Reframing

Reframing is a cognitive technique that involves changing the way an individual perceives, interprets, or frames a situation, thought, or emotion. The goal is to shift one's perspective to promote a more positive or constructive outlook, leading to changes in feelings, behaviors, or attitudes.

Benefits of Reframing

Reframing situations into a more positive and productive outlook leads to…

- stress reduction
- improved problem solving
- enhanced resilience
- better emotional regulation
- positive communication
- increased optimism
- reduced anxiety
- increased self-esteem
- empowerment over thoughts and reactions
- improved decision making
- improved well-being

AND MORE!

Tips for Reframing

1. **Awareness**: Recognize negative thoughts or interpretations that may be influencing your feelings or behaviors.

2. **Challenge Assumptions**: Question the accuracy of your initial interpretation. Consider alternative viewpoints or explanations for the situation.

3. **Language Matters**: Pay attention to the language you use to describe events. Choose words that are neutral or positive rather than overly negative.

4. **Focus on Solutions**: Shift your focus from the problem to potential solutions. What actions can you take to improve the situation?

5. **Learn from Setbacks**: View setbacks as opportunities for growth. Identify lessons learned and consider how challenges can contribute to personal development.

6. **Practice Gratitude**: Reflect on positive aspects of a situation. What are the things you can be thankful for, even in difficult circumstances?

8. **Consider the Bigger Picture**: Zoom out and look at the situation in the context of your life as a whole. Will this matter in the long run?

9. **Empathy**: Consider other people's perspectives. How might they see the situation? Understanding different viewpoints can aid in reframing.

10. **Positive Self-Talk**: Replace negative self-talk with positive and encouraging self-talk that focuses on your strengths.

Remember that reframing is a skill that improves with practice. It's about cultivating a mindset that promotes resilience, positive thinking, and adaptive responses to life's challenges.